Mums and Dads

Mum is a bus driver.

SCHOOL

Dad is a window cleaner.

Mum is a policewoman.

Dad is a vet.

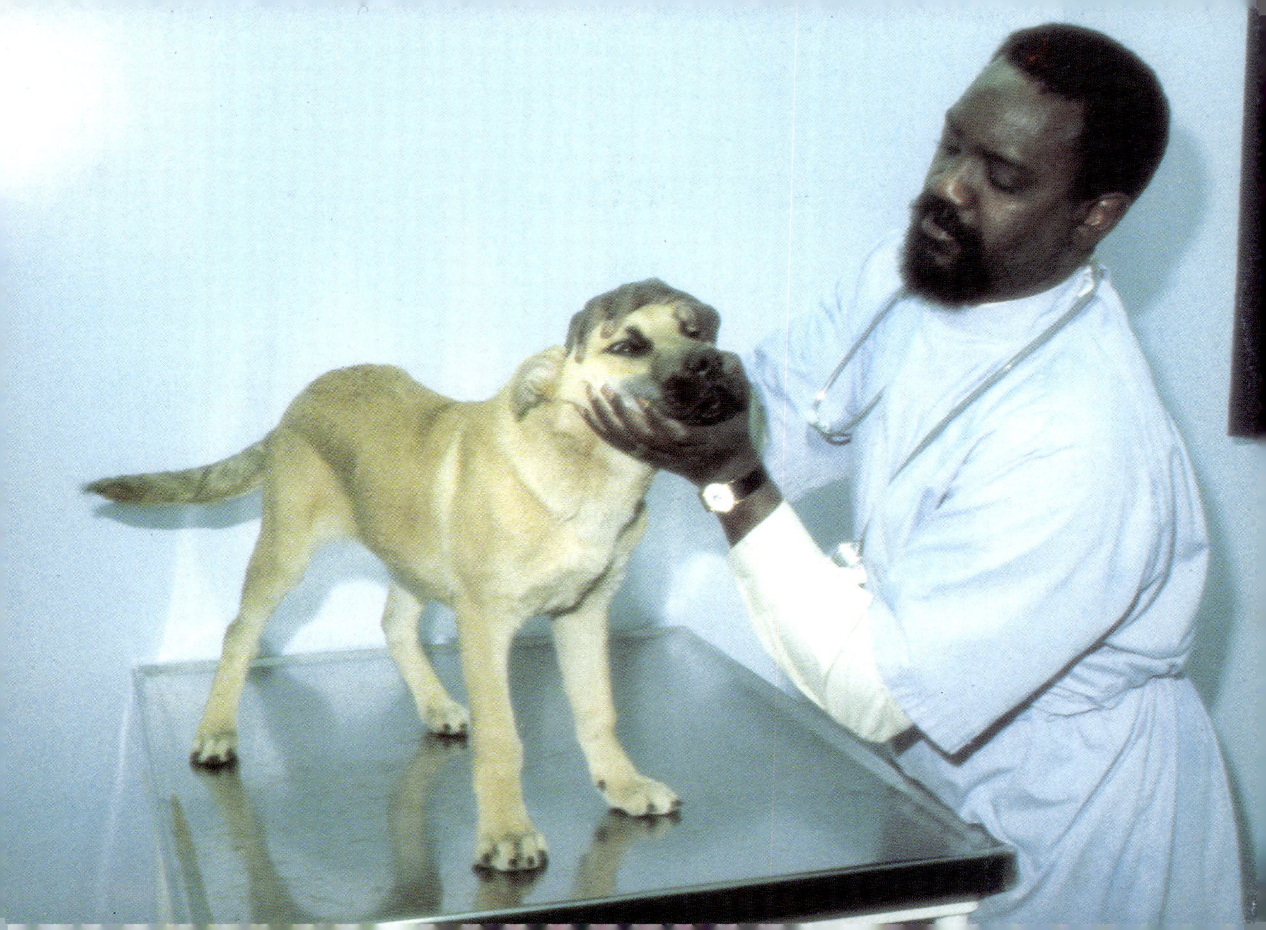

Mum is a teacher.

The Troll in the Hole
At The Café Splendid
Open the Door
Shirley Hughes
Eric Carle
The Very Busy Spider
Find Me a Tiger
ROALD DAHL
The Giraffe and the Pelly and Me
TRY AGAIN SALLY JANE

Dad is a builder.

Dad is a farmer.

Mum is a farmer, too.